Steam Memories

No. 62: Nottingham to Mansi
and on to Worksop

Along the route of the present day Robin Hood Railway line

Bill Taylor

Copyright Book Law Publications 2013

ISBN 978-1-907094-21-7

INTRODUCTION

The railway between Nottingham ands Worksop is today known as the Robin Hood line along which an hourly interval service is operated by East Midlands Trains. Following the withdrawal of steam hauled passenger trains in October 1964 nearly all the track remained in daily use thanks to the prodigious output of the deep coal mines adjacent to the route which was a source of traffic until the coal industry started to be run down after 1985. Therefore when the proposal to restore a rail service to Mansfield was being considered about 90% of the track was still in place.

This book, however, is not about the line as we know it in the 21st century, nor is it intended to be a formal history of the line. Its purpose is simply to take a look back at locations along its route in an album which shows what it looked like mainly in the 1950s and 1960s, no more no less.

Today coal trains are relatively few and far between but it is due to the country's continuing need for coal that the line survived at all. These photographs look back to the time when they outnumbered passenger workings perhaps by as many as ten to one and we must all be grateful that the photographers whose work is reproduced here chose to desert some more popular locations occasionally and bequeath to us this opportunity to admire their recordings of local railway scenes fifty or more years ago.

I hope you may enjoy this latest offering in the "Steam Memories" series of books.

Bill Taylor.   February 2013

(*Cover photograph*)   Ivatt 2-6-0 No. 46501 gets into its stride with an excursion as it thunders past Mansfield North Junction. *Frank Ashley.*

(*Title page*)   The weather in Mansfield on Bank Holiday Monday in August 1955 was "cloudy medium". Local resident and renowned railway photographer Jack Cupit so noted his records as he captured ex-LMS "Crab" 2-6-0 No. 42823 backing onto the stock of "The Mansfield Holiday Express" at 9.45am. At least it was not raining thus giving hope to those on board the train that it might be sunny by the time they reached their destination. Mansfield shed regularly borrowed this class of engine from Burton-on-Trent for excursions. *J.Cupit.*

Printed and bound by The Amadeus Press, Cleckheaton, West Yorkshire

First published in the United Kingdom by Book Law Publications, 382 Carlton Hill, Nottingham, NG4 1JA

Nottingham. To the east of Midland station London Road Junction signal box controls the lines to and from the carriage sidings as Class 3P 2-6-2 tank No. 40096 brings the empty stock of a Mansfield line service the short distance towards the platforms. Beyond the tank wagons part of the ex-GNR London Road Low Level station remains in use, though no longer for passenger trains. *D.Lawrence.*

Nottingham. For the first ten years following the Grouping of 1923 ex-Midland Railway 0-4-4T locomotives operated the majority of passenger trains between Mansfield and Worksop but when Stanier introduced his 3 cylinder 2-6-4T engines for use between Fenchurch Street and Southend the native Tilbury line locomotives had to be deployed elsewhere. Several were reallocated to Nottingham and Mansfield sheds theoretically to provide the crews with stronger motive power. On 25 May 1935 Class 2P 4-4-2T No. 2102 (later 41920) still carrying Westinghouse equipment arrives at platform 3 from Mansfield sporting express headlights. *V.Forster*.

Nottingham.   The Johnson 0-4-4T locomotives were used for many years on branch line passenger trains throughout for former Midland Railway system. Although this photograph is well known it is worthy of inclusion as it shows a train typical of those operating on all the lines radiating from the Mansfield area in the early years of the LMS. This view in March 1933 shows No. 1327 of Derby shed waiting in the middle road. It was withdrawn from service in 1940. *T.G.Hepburn.*

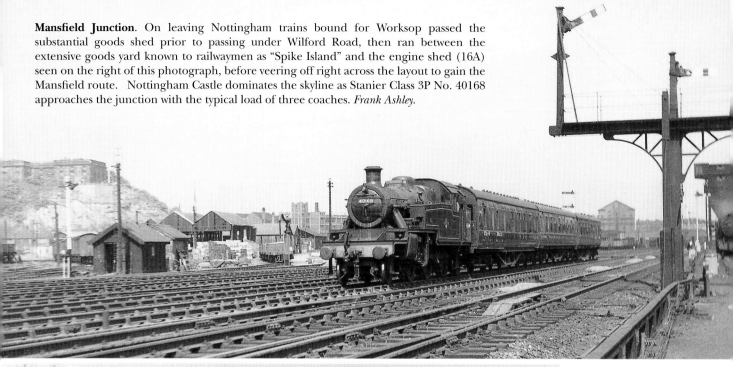

Mansfield Junction. On leaving Nottingham trains bound for Worksop passed the substantial goods shed prior to passing under Wilford Road, then ran between the extensive goods yard known to railwaymen as "Spike Island" and the engine shed (16A) seen on the right of this photograph, before veering off right across the layout to gain the Mansfield route. Nottingham Castle dominates the skyline as Stanier Class 3P No. 40168 approaches the junction with the typical load of three coaches. *Frank Ashley*.

Lenton. An early twentieth century view of Lenton North Junction looking towards Basford. The line going off to the left enabled trains from the Leen Valley pits to reach Beeston Sidings. *Author collection*.

Radford. The first major junction along the Mansfield line lies immediately at the platform end and is appropriately named Radford Junction. The line to Trowell on the Erewash Valley route goes off behind the signal box whilst ahead the factory chimneys of Basford beckon in the distance. This mixed train from the Erewash Valley line clatters over the points hauled by 3F 0-6-0 No. 43825 whose shedplate indicates it was allocated to Westhouses. *D.B.Swale.*

Radford. A commendably clean Class 8F 2-8-0 No. 48675 of Nottingham shed has charge of a Kirkby Sidings to Wellingborough coal train in this 1958 view. To reach its destination there was a choice of routes one via Nottingham and Melton Mowbray, the other via Leicester. *C.A. Hill.*

Near Radford.   Between Radford Junction and Basford was a section of track where loops existed on both sides of the line.   In this 1959 view the exhaust suggests that the fireman is busy using his shovel while the driver has clearly noticed the photographer as he coaxes Stanier 3P No. 40184 along the lower Leen valley. *C.A.Hill.*

Bobber's Mill. When the Nottingham to Kirkby-in-Ashfield line was built in the 1840s no fewer than ten roads were crossed on the level before Hucknall was reached, but most of these became a nuisance to road vehicles in the last century so as time went by they were replaced by bridges spanning the line. The level crossing at Bobber's Mill on what is now the A610 main road must have been very troublesome, but this view taken on 25 January 1931 shows foundations and stanchions being erected to carry the overbridge which would soon eliminate the problem. An audience has gathered to watch the proceedings. *Courtesy of Nottingham City Council and www.picturethepast.org.uk.*

Basford. Basford's factory chimneys preside over the scene on 9 June 1962 when the goods yard offered a variety of wagons which would do justice to any model railway layout. Apart from a few weeds between the nearest tracks the railway premises look quite tidy in this delightful view of "Crab" 2-6-0 No. 42763 engaging in a spot of shunting but looking fit to tackle any job required of it.

Milepost 92 –railphotolibrary.com/HenryPriestley

Basford. Stanier 4P 2-6-4T No. 42618 slows for the Basford stop but passengers are notable by their absence. Perhaps they are going by road as two Nottingham Corporation trolley buses are in view as well as Trent Motor Traction service 61 to Mansfield trying to keep pace with the train and meeting another of its kind going towards the city. *Author collection.*

Above.

Bulwell. An early morning train from Nottingham sets off from the station on 30 March 1959. No. 40168 was a long standing resident of Mansfield shed giving service till the end of 1961. *J. Cupit.*

Left:

Bulwell. Now looking in the opposite direction four passengers wait for the next train going north. The totem proclaims the full station name of Bulwell Market. *H. C. Casserley.*

Bulwell. Stanier 2-6-2T No. 40073 gets away from Bulwell on 20 June 1961, the penultimate stop on its journey from Worksop. Except for the Parish Church virtually nothing remains of this scene today as the tram system occupies the formation of the down line and the Robin Hood line is a bi-directional single track at this point. *J. Cupit*

Above:

Bulwell Forest. With a rake of what at the time were considered to be high capacity mineral wagons returning to Newstead Colliery Class 8F No. 48214, having passed beneath the blue brick viaduct constructed by the GCR in the 1890s, makes steady progress up the grade on 12 July 1963. Little evidence remains of the viaduct today but the Robin Hood line now keeps company with the Nottingham tram system at this point. *B.W.L.Brooksbank.*

Right:

Bestwood Junction. On 27 April 1957 B.R. Standard 2-6-2T No. 84006 working a railtour which included a trip along the branch to Calverton Colliery pauses to quench its thirst alongside more familiar motive power in the shape of Class 8F No. 48748 which waits patiently for the stranger to leave. Today you will find Moorbridge tramstop hereabouts. *R. J. Buckley.*

Butler's Hill.   There is a tram stop here today but the Midland Railway did not see fit to provide a station, unlike the Great Northern Company whose establishment is visible beyond the bridge. The two lines ran very close to each other here, the darkened portions of the bridge revealing their respective positions.   Two signal boxes can just be seen, the MR Hucknall No. 2 cabin being just to the left of the telegraph pole. *Author collection*.

Hucknall. Photographs of Hucknall station seem hard to come by possibly because the surroundings were not particularly attractive. This view taken on 5 May 1962 shows the second station which the Midland Railway provided for the town when development of the coal mines rendered the original premises inconvenient. Plans were drawn up and contracts were let in 1894 for the new station which was designed as an island platform as seen here. The colliery sidings on the right are now the site of the tram terminus while all signs of the colliery itself have been eradicated to be replaced by a car park and a Tesco superstore. *milepost92 –railphotolibrary.com/HenryPriestley*.

Linby. The photographer is shielded by the Down platform canopy in this LMS period view showing the principal station buildings on the opposite side of the line where the platform surface is noticeably low. The original cabin controlled more than just the level crossing gates because the crossover in the foreground was the start of the access to Linby Colliery's sidings. Space was precious so a replacement platform for Nottingham bound trains was added just north of the road crossing. *D. Thompson*.

Linby.   During the final month of steam hauled passenger trains along the line Stanier 2-6-4T No.42588 pauses at Linby's Up platform. The parallel ex GNR line passes below the other bridge on the ex GCR line which is at the higher level.   Maybe the elderly gentleman has come to have a last look at the station prior to closure. *Author collection.*

Newstead.   Young children from the adjacent colliery village play apparently unsupervised on the station platform.   I hope their parents know where they are!   This view looks towards Mansfield. *Author collection.*

Newstead. Who says the Mansfield trains were never dieselised? True, the railcars never materialised, though some say they were promised by BR and destination blinds showing MANSFIELD were reputedly seen a few years before passenger trains ceased to run. Only one week to go as train 2D41 rolls into the station with D.5224 in charge on 3 October 1964. This surprising motive power may have been the result of a steam locomotive failing and Nottingham shed being unable to find any other substitute. *Author.*

ANNESLEY STATION. M.R. 3

Annesley. The station here was surrounded by railway lines and sidings of other companies and of the pits to say nothing of the GCR engine shed and wagon works, the local colliery and its attendant spoil heap. Most of the houses hereabouts were at Annesley Woodhouse some distance away for which this station was especially inconvenient. The colliery village comprised the few dwellings known as Annesley Rows, but their occupiers could reach Newstead station on foot in less than ten minutes. No wonder then that Annesley saw its last passenger train as early as April 1952. *Author collection.*

Kirkby Tunnel. The transition from steam to diesel traction was well advanced by May 1966 when this photograph was taken, but the control of a heavy coal train made up of unbraked wagons down the incline between Kirkby and the environs of Nottingham demanded both skill of the driver and sufficient brake power of the locomotive. Brush Type 4 diesel D.1829 has the benefit of two brake tenders and Class 8F No. 48303 to assist the descent as it approaches the tunnel under the Robin Hood hills. *J. S. Hancock.*

Kirkby Tunnel. The foliage on both sides of the track suggest this early 1950s photograph was taken in early summer.   A venerable ex- London Tilbury & Southend Railway tank locomotive No. 41940 having negotiated the 199 yard tunnel wheezes past Kirkby Station Junction's fixed distant signal thankful that it has won the battle with the steeper gradient north of Hucknall. *Frank Ashley.*

Kirkby-in-Ashfield. The 4.16pm Saturdays only trains from Mansfield often had two engines up front, but purely to save a light engine movement for a Nottingham based locomotive. Class 2P 4-4-0 No. 40553 sports the ordinary passenger headlamp as it shares the job with a Stanier 2-6-2 tank, seen here passing Kingsway Park, locally known as The Acre. *Frank Ashley.*

Kirkby-in-Ashfield. One of the larger variety of ex - LT&SR tank engines No. 41940 sets off for Nottingham in this early 1950s view. For many years the endless procession of trains over Station Street's level crossing, many of them slow moving coal trains, held up the traffic. Pedestrians could use the footbridge but it was not unusual for motor vehicles (and cycles) to have to wait ten minutes or even longer. *Frank Ashley.*

Kirkby Shed. Proposals to sink more coal mines along the Nottinghamshire/Derbyshire border north of Mansfield in the 1890s as well as developments in Yorkshire after 1900 beyond Shireoaks caused the Midland Company to consider where it should accommodate the substantial number of additional engines it would require to work the extra trains. Mansfield shed did not lend itself to being extended, so the solution was to build a new three road affair of typical pitch roof design at Kirkby which it completed in 1903 to house fifteen 0-6-0 goods locomotives. By 1935 we observe from this picture that engines of that wheel arrangement still dominated the scene.

Author collection.

Kirkby Shed. By 1950 the facilities at Kirkby were woefully inadequate for by now the complement had swelled to more than sixty locomotives of which about two thirds were of Class 8F. Rather late in the day BR made an effort to improve the situation by adding a new two road building in 1958 alongside the original Midland Railway shed, and replacing the old coaler with overhead delivery as well as installing an ash plant with narrow gauge lines to deliver the tubs. Even so only half the engines were under cover at weekends and in the space of ten years the entire site was redundant. No. 48405 and other class 8Fs occupy the shed yard about 1962. *D. Dykes.*

Kirkby Sidings. Time is running out for steam traction but there is still plenty of coal to be moved out of the sidings. The 4Fs have gone for scrap so the pilot engine to hold this Toton bound train in check as it descends the line to Pye Bridge is a Class 8F, as is the the locomotive attached to the wagons. No. 48346 looks down at heel with tender half empty, shed code 16E painted hap-hazardly on the smokebox door, and cladding around the firebox apparently loose. Behind, No. 48284 is just as grime covered but hopefully in better shape. *Author collection.*

Kirkby Summit. The distant signal is pulled off indicating that this excursion train has a clear road to take the Pye Bridge line beyond Kirkby station. Class 4F No. 43885 is passing the Up sidings with the sprawl of Summit Colliery on the opposite side of the line. The date is 5 September 1959. *D. Dykes.*

Kirkby Hardwick. In 1963 LNER Class B1 No. 61013 TOPI brings coal from Shirebrook past Kirkby Hardwick, now the location of Sutton Parkway on the Robin Hood line.

J. S. Hancock.

Kirkby-in-Ashfield. Granted this image is of poor quality but against that must be taken into consideration that it is a wartime view when film was hard to obtain, heavy snow had fallen in February 1942 and the photographer must have taken a risk. Class 8F No. 8214 is passing Kirkby Station Junction's Down starting signal with a very late running 8.15am Mansfield to Nottingham train and there is no steam heating by the look of the carriages. *J. Robinson.*

Sutton Junction. The safety valves are lifting on 8F No. 48267 as it passes the tidy but almost deserted station with a heavy train load of coal in April 1963. *Author.*

Sutton Junction. The 11.46am Nottingham to Worksop train glides into the station on a sunny 14 September 1963 with Fairburn 2-6-4T No. 42218 at the head. By this date Sutton Junction was the last survivor of Sutton's four railway stations though it was furthest from the centre of town. In previous years the branch to the former Midland Railway terminus in Sutton went off to the right beyond the water tower. Are those "beatle boots" the lads are wearing? Top of the charts at the time was "She loves you..." by.....you know who! *J. Cupit.*

Sutton Junction. On Saturdays an additional train was put on from Nottingham as far as Mansfield to cater for city workers who worked a half day. Taken the same day as the previous photograph another Fairburn engine No. 42232 is in charge of this working due at 1.3pm according to the timetable but only just ready to depart at 1.20pm as noted by the photographer. *J. Cupit.*

Sutton Junction. With a tank locomotive at the head it was quite common to work bunker first going south as in this view of No. 42221 looking for trade on 1 June 1963. The tall chimney was part of Adlington's Mill which once had its own siding, whilst the factory roof above the coaches was camouflaged during the second world war to protect the foundry workers at Stokes, Taylor & Shaw from overhead attack. *R. J. Buckley.*

Sutton-in-Ashfield. Opened for passenger trains on 3 May 1893 the short branch from the junction station ascended on a gradient of 1 in 66 to this terminus much closer to the town, but had a chequered existence with the service being suspended more than once before finally ending in October 1951 when only one daily train in each direction ran. On account of the fare the train was christened "penny emma" and, as in this 1941 view was invariably in the hands of a Johnson 0-4-4T, in this instance No. 1297. *H. C. Casserley.*

Sutton Forest. On 17 September 1963 Stanier Class 4P No. 42629 crosses Coxmoor Road with the 6.18pm service from Mansfield to Nottingham. The house on the right was built by the Midland Railway shortly after it acquired the Mansfield & Pinxton Railway line in 1847 and remains in use as a dwelling today. The siding gave access to a refrigerated warehouse used as a food distribution depot in the second world war. *Author.*

Left:

Kings Mill. Now a Grade II listed structure and claiming to be the oldest railway viaduct in England having been built as part of the Mansfield & Pinxton line in 1817, a footpath crosses it today although until 1970 it carried rails and was used as a siding for wagon storage. *Author*.

Right:

Bleak Hills. In 1872 the Midland Railway constructed a deviation line to ease the curvature of the line near to Kings Mill thus relegating the former M&P trackbed to a siding. The work required the construction of a timber viaduct with masonry approach as seen in this view taken at the time. Midland Railway distance diagrams show it as "Bleak Hills (Wooden) viaduct No. 25" at 139m 38ch. *Author collection*.

Bleak Hills. Apparently taken before the 1923 Grouping this view of Midland Railway 4-4-0 No. 373 crossing the Bleak Hills viaduct behind Hermitage Mill depicts a rural scene despite being so close to the town of Mansfield. It is believed that when the structure was in need of repair in early LMS days wagons loaded with rock and spoil were discharged over both sides of the structure until an embankment was formed to carry the permanent way. *Author collection.*

Mansfield South Junction.   The view looking south from the signal box on 8 May 1965 as BR Standard Class 9F No. 92155 approaches with an enthusiasts special working bound for Doncaster.   *Author.*

Mansfield South Junction. The milepost denotes the commencement of the single line branch to Southwell and Rolleston Junction turning away beyond the signal box. The roof of Mansfield shed is visible above the train although by the time this photograph was taken on 8 August 1964 the track leading to it in the fork of the two running lines had been removed. LMS Class 5 No. 45253, a locomotive which took part in the 1948 locomotive exchanges, approaches with the Skegness to Radford working. *Milepost92 railphotolibrary.comHenryPriestley.*

Mansfield shed. The depot offers a variety of LMS motive power in this view from the 1950s. From left to right the four shed roads are occupied by Hughes "Crab" No. 42760 no doubt borrowed for an excursion, Class 4F No. 44394 useful for goods or local passenger work, Tilbury tank No. 41943 well coaled and ready to ply between Nottingham and Worksop if no more than four coaches are attached, and Class 8F No. 48156 a long-time resident accustomed to dealing with the important coal traffic of the district. *Author collection.*

Mansfield shed. Recently arrived at Mansfield this small ex. LT&SR tank No. 2099 rests by the coaling stage while the driver attends to the necessary lubrication.   Could that be the fireman on high manually filling the bunker with coal?   Although intended to be an improvement on the Johnson 0-4-4T engines used on the passenger turns, the larger driving wheels of these locomotives were not ideal on the 1 in 70 rising gradient north of Hucknall. They were not popular with footplatemen, partly because the cabs were both hot and cramped. *H.C. Casserley.*

Mansfield North Junction. Taken from the footbridge adjacent to Cinderella Walk the overall roof of the town's station can be made out in the distance as a 2-6-4T makes a brisk start on a Nottingham service and meets an equally anonymous 4F returning empty wagons to one of the local pits.   The Mansfield Co-operative Society warehouse on Victoria Street is partly concealed by steam from the goods engine, whilst the line trailing in from the right is from the Southwell line via Mansfield East Junction. *D. Dykes.*

Mansfield North Junction. On 29 September 1962 Class 8F No. 48224 brings a mixed freight out of the goods yard and takes the Nottingham line at the junction. It may have been assigned to the service which departed about 6.25pm picking up a few wagons at Kirkby. The engine then went on shed after arrival in Nottingham where it turned and took on water ready to return from Spike Island goods yard behind the last passenger train of the day. *Author*.

Mansfield North Junction. A wide high level view looking north reveals something of the extent of the sidings at Mansfield. The main goods shed is adjacent to the station buildings in the distance. Class 4F No. 44268 is busy shunting. The sidings on the right are only reached from a point on the line between here and Mansfield East Junction. *J. Cupit.*

Mansfield. A view which needs no comment beyond saying the station had everything you would expect given the population of the town. *Stations UK.*

Mansfield. On a sunny day in June 1955 Class 3F No. 43727 assists a Class 8F up the grade with a Shirebrook Sidings – Toton coal train. To the right is platform 3 and beyond it the goods shed. In the years before the reincarnation as the Robin Hood line the main station buildings had seen several uses, including a night club most inappropriately called Brunels! *D. Thompson.*

Mansfield. A view of the main entrance to the station when the maroon enamel signs so much sought by collectors of railway artefacts were present. They have all gone along with the telephone box and the gas lamp, but happily the structure is still relatively intact where the facilities include a booking office. *Nevis*.

Left:

Mansfield. Ivatt Class 4MT 2-6-0 No. 43145 takes on water while working the "Dukeries" railtour on 24 July 1960 allowing its patrons to stretch their legs. *RCTS*.

Right:

Mansfield. The dock at the south end of platform 1 provides a suitable vantage point to capture on film Class 5 No. 44869 about to leave with the 8.20am excursion to Southport (maybe for the Flower Show?) on 8 August 1962. *Author*.

Mansfield viaduct. This masonry viaduct, constructed in 1875 when the extension to Worksop was finally completed, still dominates part of the town and has been professionally cleaned in recent years. The nearest building on the left was once the town's lunatic asylum, and beyond that Queen Street goes off to the left while the road behind the four storey shop leads down to the market place. Note the white circles on the MR pattern signal arms. *Author collection.*

Mansfield. Looking south along platform 2 this May 1953 view portrays the station as a bright and airy place albeit not very busy. *D. Thompson.*

Mansfield. Station North signal box is almost completely obscured by Class 4F No. 44416 arriving from Worksop about 1955. Five coaches may have been asking too much of a Tilbury tank! *Frank Ashley*.

Above:
Mansfield Woodhouse. The station as built in 1875 was an attractive timber construction with general design and accommodation similar to the masonry buildings on the stations further north along the route. The use of timber may have been to take account of land subsidence due to coal mining as the platforms were of similar material. The goods shed in the middle distance was sympathetically converted in the 1990s to form part of the present day station on the Robin Hood line. *Author collection.*

Left:
Mansfield Woodhouse. Some 87 years later the main building looks to be in good order. Not much has changed though the platform now has an asphalt surface. *Author.*

Near Mansfield Woodhouse. Going south chimney first Stanier Class 3P No. 40175 has four coaches in tow on a sunny afternoon in March 1956. *Author collection*.

Above:

Pleasley Junction. The 1.30pm Saturday service from Worksop to Mansfield drifts past Pleasley Junction signal box on 12 October 1963 behind Stanier Class 4P No. 42587. The line on the left gave access to Pleasley where one line continued to Westhouses and, in earlier years, another veered north via Bolsover. In 1904 passenger trains ran along both of those routes. Does anyone know of a photograph of Rowthorn station? *Milepost92 railphotolibrary.com/HenryPriestley.*

Left:

Shirebrook Colliery Platform. This platform was provided on the west side of the line for the use of miners. Here it is being passed by Class 5 No. 45282 with a Nottingham to Cleethorpes excursion on 3 August 1965. *R. J. Buckley.*

55

Shirebrook. Looking south from the road bridge the spoil heaps of Shirebrook Colliery occupy both sides of the line as "Crab" 2-6-0 No. 42896 arrives on 11 June 1957. This train originated at Radford and would leave the Worksop route immediately on departure to continue its journey via Edwinstowe and Lincoln. The goods shed would later be incorporated into the diesel depot which once existed here. *R. J. Buckley.*

Shirebrook. In May 1963 No. 42587 puts in another appearance with a southbound ordinary service train at Shirebrook where business seems brisk. The signals at the end of the Up platform protect Shirebrook Junction where the line to Warsop swings to the right just beyond the road overbridge. *D. Loveday.*

Shirebrook. Summer Saturday holiday trains were very popular in the 1950s and early 1960s and, being well supported, often ran to ten vehicles and therefore requiring larger engines which the local sheds could not provide. BR Standard Class 4 No. 75062 has nine coaches forming the return from Yarmouth Vauxhall which terminates here. The date is 26 August 1961. *D. Holmes.*

Shirebrook. Rarely, if ever, had Fowler designed 2-6-2T locomotives been seen on Mansfield line trains, that is until two of them arrived unexpectedly from Scotland. The pair, Nos. 40050 and 40054, did provide a bit of variety although whether they were any better than the Stanier versions which they worked alongside is a moot point. No. 40050 calls on 16 April 1960 with the 1.33pm from Worksop. *R. J. Buckley.*

Shirebrook Junction. Reporting number M954 relates to a Clay Cross to Skegness special train seen approaching from the north. The train will have been routed via Chesterfield, Foxlow Junction, Clowne and Elmton & Creswell and is headed by 3F No. 43211 assisting 4F No, 44212. A reversal will now take place and, with a fresh Eastern Region engine in charge, the train will take the line on the right to join the former Lancashire, Derbyshire & East Coast Railway line to Lincoln going on via Woodhall Spa to reach the coast. The date is 22 August 1951 when the connection to Shirebrook North was still in place. Known locally as the "New Found Out" the Down line climbs steeply above the 4F while the signals for the Up connection of this flying junction are seen at danger above the roof of the signal box. *R. J. Buckley.*

Shirebrook Junction. An official view of the layout taken by the MR photographer with the points and signals set for a train from Langwith Junction, later to be called Shirebrook North. *Author collection.*

Shirebrook Cutting. To the north of Shirebrook the line passed through a limestone cutting and turned towards the village of Langwith. In order to serve Welbeck Colliery a branch line was constructed by the LMS in 1928, which involved further excavation as is evident in this view of Hughes 2-6-0 No. 42767 passing the connection with a Worksop to Buxton excursion on 7 April 1958. The colliery branch was short-lived, opening in January 1929 and being taken out of use on 2 November 1959. *R. J. Buckley.*

Langwith cutting. Two days after a rather damp Coronation Day in 1953 a hazy sun throws some light on Tilbury tank No. 41947 and on the penny daisies in the cutting. *R. J. Buckley.*

Above:

Langwith. Nottingham shed has turned out one of its Fowler 2-6-4T locos, No. 42333, for the first Down service of the day seen here returning with the 8.15am train from Worksop having just left the station. The building in the background is Langwith Maltings, the premises for many years of S. Peach & Co. Ltd., served by a short siding on the west side of the main line. *R. J. Buckley.*

Right:

Langwith. Langwith station gets a visit from Class 3P No., 41961 working the 9.40am Nottingham to Worksop service on 21 August 1951. The milepost hides its information from us but the engine driver could see that it showed 124.5 miles from St. Pancras. *R. J. Buckley.*

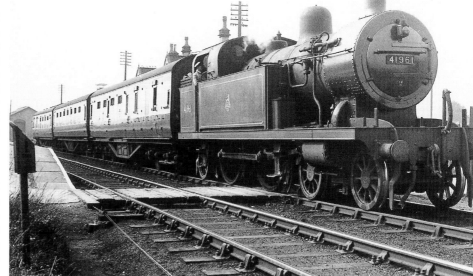

Langwith. By keeping the approaching train in the distance we are afforded an overall view of the main station buildings, constructed in limestone to satisfy the landed gentry of the nearby Dukeries area, as they appeared on 19 March 1955. W.D. 2-8-0 No. 90729 is tender first with a rake of mineral wagons. Perhaps these engines "nosed" from side to side rather less when going backwards?

Milepost92 railphotolibrary.com/HenryPriestley.

Near Langwith. Six coaches demands a tender locomotive which Mansfield shed has rostered for a Whitwell to Nottingham run on 14 October 1950. Class 3F No. 43634 has cleared the station area as it accelerates away. The goods shed and the access to Langwith Maltings are seen on the left where three wagons occupy the yard. The outline of Langwith Colliery tip can be made out above the stock. *R. J. Buckley.*

Elmton & Creswell. Standard pattern station buildings were erected here although ornately finished with terra cotta ridge tiles and decorative timber fascias. The banner signals operated by the LMS style signal box denote the junction of the steeply graded line to Clown and Staveley. *D. Thompson.*

Elmton & Creswell. On 6 January 1962 a bit of snow lies on the ground and it must still be cold, witness the passengers with hands in pockets of their winter coats. Stanier Class 4P No. 42618 makes a worthwhile call with the 1.33pm train from Worksop. *R. J. Buckley.*

Near Creswell.   One of the last surviving ex MR Class 4F 0-6-0 engines was brought down to the Midlands from the Barrow-in-Furness area and specially groomed before working this special train organised by the Railway Correspondence and Travel Society.   Most of the itinerary was in the East Midlands and here it has climbed the short rise from Elmton & Creswell and is seen passing the splendid distant signal applicable to trains going the other way along the single line section. *Author*.

Whitwell Tunnel. Having passed through this 544 yard tunnel Class 4F No. 44139 slows on the approach to the station with the 8.40am service from Nottingham on 1 June 1963 comprising three vehicles which appear to have come straight out of the carriage works. *R.J.Buckley.*

Whitwell. By standing on the road overbridge this overall view of the railway scene looking south has been obtained for us to enjoy. Fairburn Class 4 tank No. 42232 pauses with the 9.45am from Nottingham in October 1962. *R.J.Buckley.*

Whitwell. LNER O2 2-8-0 No. 63986 of Retford shed backs a line of empty mineral wagons for Whitwell Colliery past the signal box in June 1963. The station is seen in the distance. *R.J.Buckley.*

Whitwell. On 1 August 1964 BR Standard Class 2 No. 78055 accelerates away from the station with an Up local passenger working. To the north of Whitwell lay Steetley Colliery where lime works were also established. The containers in the goods yard were used to transport away the finely crushed lime for use in making cement. *R.J.Buckley.*

Whitwell. Class B1 No. 61212 was a Retford engine for many years, often found in a siding just north of Retford station facing south acting as pilot, and affectionately known by trainspotters as "Retford Rocket". Proof that it sometimes performed other work is found in this view of the locomotive in commendably clean condition heading a special excursion to Belle Vue on 23 April 1962. *R.J.Buckley.*

Near Shireoaks Junctions. This view of LMS Fowler 2-6-4T No. 2308 taken about 1930 shows typical pre-Grouping rolling stock used on the line at the time. It is believed that the engine was allocated to Nottingham shed. *P. Ransome-Wallis.*

Near Shireoaks Junctions. By way of contrast to the previous illustration Mansfield shed has turned out Johnson 0-4-4T No. 1309. *P. Ransome-Wallis.*

Woodend Junction. The points are negotiated by Class 4P No. 42221 as it takes the Worksop line on 22 August 1964 with the 3.20pm train from Mansfield Woodhouse. *Milepost92 railphotolibrary.com/HenryPriestley.*

Worksop. Class B1 No. 61094 approaches the east end of the station with a stopping train for Sheffield on 6 June 1962 and passes Class 4P No. 42628 which has run round its stock and reversed a short distance beyond the level crossing. It will shortly use the crossover to reach platform 1 to form the 8.5pm departure for Nottingham. *Author*.

Worksop. The mock Jacobean style of architecture of this station is glimpsed above the platform awning in this pleasant study of Johnson 0-4-4T No. 1342 waiting to leave with a train for the Mansfield line. A comparison with the locomotive on page 76 will reveal detail differences. *P. Ransome-Wallis.*

Worksop. The final picture is of Fairburn tank No. 42231 which, having run round its train stands in platform 1 ready to return to Nottingham. Observe the lightweight DMU standing alongside on a Lincoln service. It was a pity these diesel units were never used between here and Nottingham. Mansfield was the second largest town in the county and said to be the largest town in England without a rail passenger service after October 1964. *Author.*

LONDON TRANSPORT BUSES

A Colour Portfolio

R. C. Riley

Ian Allan
PUBLISHING

Introduction

This book sets out to portray the London bus scene as it was in the 1970s. The area covered consists mainly of the City, the West End and South East London. The Central Area photographs were taken usually during my lunch hour — sometimes a bit extended. The regular sorties to places like the Gloucester Road Air Terminal for Heathrow Airport were connected to flights to and from Europe on business. The area served by London buses was and is so large that I felt the need to specialise and concentrate my attention on the areas mentioned above.

My interest in London buses goes back a long way. In my extreme youth I remember in particular six-wheeled buses — the small LS class that I could see at Victoria on route 16 and those operated by the City Bus Company, one of the more respectable 'pirates' whose six-wheeled Leylands could be seen on routes 536 and 537. Another independent operator whose buses I used to see was C. H. Pickup of Dulwich, whose fleet was sufficiently modern to provide five STL-class buses to the LPTB on its formation in 1933. I attended school in Holborn and this gave me the opportunity to see many former independent Leylands then classed TD in service on route 18, often in their original livery. I was studying Latin at the time so perhaps that explains why the names *Pro Bono Publico* and *Nil Desperandum* are now recalled. In the late 1930s I came across some 20 TDs huddled together in a yard off Effra Road, Brixton, presumably awaiting disposal. What a pity I never pointed my Box Brownie at any of these. One thing I do recall is that the 'pirates' were quicker in fitting pneumatic tyres to their buses than LGOC.

Other bus journeys that I recall include visiting my maternal grandparents, who lived in Caterham Valley. This entailed a 68 bus from Tulse Hill to South Croydon 'Red Deer', thence a 75 bus operated by Thomas Tilling. The screen behind the driver carried the words 'THIS IS A PETROL ELECTRIC BUS AND DOES NOT JERK WHEN STARTING'. Maybe not, but it jerked at most other times. Then there was an aunt at Lee, who could be reached by a No 2 bus to Crystal Palace, thence one of the extraordinary NS 'tunnel buses' on route 108, in which everyone sat facing one another. My father was a Member of the Zoological Society, which meant a good many journeys to Regents Park Zoo, easily reached by a route 169 bus, now severely truncated and known as route 196. Both the 68 and the 169 went past Euston station, and from the top deck I could admire the crimson boiler-tops of engines on the arrival side. That settled the matter, and I became a railway photographer.

Front cover: Winter sunshine on Crystal Palace Parade gives a clear picture of RT4007 on route 122 and RM2079 on route 137, photographed on 28 December 1971.

Rear cover: On a fine 6 October 1975, RF408 passes the Crossroads Inn at Shepperton on its way to Kingston on route 218.

Title page: My first LT bus photograph came about by chance. I had left my office mid-morning to view the arrival of HMS *Belfast* in the Pool of London in May 1955. There was an unexpected traffic hold-up — I know not why — and I turned to record six RT-family vehicles, with the pavement relatively free. Between RT928 on route 43 and RT3965 on route 133 there was a roofbox-fitted RT on route 35. The roof-mounted route-number box was discontinued on new construction at the end of 1948 and the last so fitted, RT1903, was withdrawn in 1971. *All photographs by the author except where stated otherwise*

First published 2001

ISBN 0 7110 2831 1

Published by Ian Allan Publishing

an imprint of Ian Allan Publishing Ltd, Hersham, Surrey KT12 4RG.
Printed by Ian Allan Printing Ltd, Hersham, Surrey KT12 4RG.

Code: 0110/B3

I am told that some of the elder statesmen of the bus-enthusiast movement were quite dismayed by the arrival in large numbers of the RT class, as this would mean the end for the ST, LT and STL classes. I can sympathise with this view, as the situation was similar to the advent of LMS-design 2-6-4 tanks built at Brighton Works and destined to replace some of the old favourites such as the LBSC 'I3'-class 4-4-2 tanks. I was little involved in the end of steam on British Railways; my wife had presented me with two fine sons in 1966 and 1968 and my camera was kept busy recording them. But

Above: Another hurried shot. On 3 June 1956 I was driving along Crystal Palace Parade in order to take a photograph of a steam-hauled Ramblers' Special at the low-level station. (The high-level station, although closed, had not yet been demolished.) I came to a hasty stop as I saw RM1 in original condition on route 2. Although built in 1954, while the RT was still in production, it did not enter passenger service until 1956. Three years later it became a training bus.

there was still a desire to record something of the transport scene and, as I found it hard to come to terms with diesels on steel rails, my attention was turned to diesels on rubber tyres. This was triggered by a visit to a traction-engine rally at Ardingly in July 1971. These were becoming Historic Commercial Vehicle events and among those present were G351, RT54, RTL343 and RTW29. It was now my turn to be dismayed; these splendid buses of the RT family, which I had seen enter service, were now on their way out. Already I was to learn that the last RTW had run in 1966 and the last RTL two years later. Fortunately I had longer than expected to record the survivors, as the new one-man buses were proving troublesome. Indeed the last surviving single-deckers of the MB and SM families were taken out of service in 1981, in which year over 300 of the new double-deck DMS class were also withdrawn. The RT had lasted in service until April 1979.

Shared between the Central and Country Areas, the RT family had eventually totalled 6,956 buses, made up of 4,825 RTs, 1,631 RTLs and 500 RTWs — a formidable total. Had the initial expectations of the Reshaping Plan to introduce one-man-operated (OMO) buses been fulfilled, the RTs would have disappeared from London streets some years earlier. As it was, their record of 40 years in service was hard to beat. However, production models of the Routemaster entered traffic in 1959 and a few hundred RMs and RMLs are still in service today. This is due chiefly to the rapid loading and unloading facilitated by their open-platform design; for this reason they are concentrated largely on routes serving the West End and the City. The Routemaster fleet delivered new to London Transport numbered 2,760, partly as a result of the need to replace trolleybuses. Other buses have come and gone in the interim, but the sight of the RMs still hard at work serves as a reminder of why I photographed buses back in the 1970s and early 1980s.

Acknowledgement is due to the publications of LOTS, notably the London Bus Magazine, to Capital Transport, to Peter Waller and his colleagues at Ian Allan, and to my wife Christine.

Above: Although I started bus photography too late to record 'prewar' RTs in service, these were still to be seen at traction-engine rallies. RT44, in a form of wartime livery, was seen at the Horsham rally on 11 September 1971, being followed by postwar Cravens-bodied RT1499 in Country Area livery. The *Picture Post* advertisements were a feature of wartime buses.

Right: Taking part in the Historic Commercial Vehicle Club London–Brighton run on 7 May 1972, RT54 was recorded approaching Streatham Hill, with wartime utility Guy Arab III G351 following. The latter vehicle (actually built in 1946) is preserved at Cobham Bus Museum.

Left: Guy Arab G351 again, seen at the Ardingly rally on 4 July 1971 together with RTL343, one of 1,631 RTLs built as modified Leyland PD2s. At the time (1947-9), AEC, traditional builder of London's buses, was having difficulty in meeting the large orders being placed by London Transport, hence the need to approach Leyland Motors, which would later take over AEC.

Above: The legal requirement for buses in London established a maximum body width of 7ft 6in. By 1949 this was increased to 8ft 0in and a further batch of Leylands were built in this form, the RTWs (Regent Type Wide). Having completed a spell in service with Osborne's of Tollesbury, RTW256 was recorded in a dealer's yard at Elephant & Castle on 4 June 1974, still in Osborne's livery; it had been converted for use as a caravan and was awaiting sale. Whether it found a buyer is unclear, but it is not known to be still in existence. Beside it was an ex-Newport Corporation Leyland PD2.

Left: In a scene remarkably devoid of other traffic or even pedestrians, RT1378 stands in Whitehall on a westbound route 11 journey on 14 May 1974, working from Dalston garage. The years 1974-7 were troubled ones: the new OMO buses were giving problems, and there was a shortage of spare parts for the open-platform buses — many in service far longer than had been anticipated — hence the regular appearance during this period of RTs on traditional RM routes. The important cross-town route 11, for example, had been RM-operated since 1966.

Above: Also recorded in Whitehall, RT4721, newly repainted and working out of Merton garage, pulls away from a stop on 5 October 1972. This bus was new to Hornchurch in 1954; of the final batch delivered, RT4722-59/61-94 were allocated to the Country Area, but most spent some years in store before entering service. By 1972, now part of the National Bus Company, the erstwhile Country Bus & Coach Department had more crew-operated buses than needed and sold 34 RTs back to London Transport. Route 77 was converted to RM operation in 1973.

Left: Having driven through the Strand on its journey from Liverpool Street to Kensington, RT1797 was photographed about to pass Charing Cross station on 25 March 1974. This important east–west route had been operated by RMs since 1963.

Above: In a traffic-free Charing Cross Road, RT2673 was recorded on route 176 to Forest Hill (having commenced its journey at Willesden) on 6 August 1972. This route had been RM-operated since 1976; its southern section had replaced tram route 62 in 1951.

Above: Working out of Stockwell garage, RT1731 is seen in Baker Street on its way to Norwood garage on 21 February 1974. This was another route considered sufficiently important to change over to RM operation in 1967, although Stockwell's RT allocation was to last a few years longer.

Right: How refreshing to see RT2501 in gleaming new paint without any advertisements as it reaches route 4's southern terminus of Waterloo on 9 June 1975. The route's northern terminus was Tufnell Park. It became normally RM-operated in 1971.

Left: RT355 on route 133 heads for Streatham garage on 24 January 1974. At the time, London Bridge was being rebuilt, and a ramp over which all traffic passed can be seen in the background.

Right: Approaching London Bridge station on 15 June 1972, RT4403 works a short turn on Moorgate–Sidcup route 21. As with route 133, this route remained RT-operated until 1975. The station suffered very serious bomb damage during the war, and the battle scars remained obvious at the time of the photograph.

Left: Having threaded its way through a quiet Cheapside, RT3332 passes St Paul's Cathedral on 4 April 1974 on route 9, upon which RMs had replaced RTs in 1963.

Right: On lengthy north–south route 141 (Wood Green–Grove Park), RT3745 passes the old entrance to the District Line at Blackfriars on 4 April 1974; RMs did not take over this route until March 1976. Both the main-line and sub-surface stations were later rebuilt.

17

Left: RT4816 takes the place of the usual Routemaster at Sloane Square on 6 September 1976. The blinds provided by Victoria (Gillingham Street) garage are clearly makeshift, using the side blind from a Routemaster in the via blind box. The southern terminus of route 137 was then normally Crystal Palace. Victoria garage closed in 1993.

Right: Route 71 used to work to the now-closed LCBS garage at Leatherhead, where RT3763 was recorded on 31 May 1975; the route became RM-operated in 1978. In recent years the service has terminated at Chessington World of Adventures.

Routes 54 and 75 became DMS-operated in April 1978 and February 1977 respectively, although the 54 had been RM-operated at weekends since 1973. Lined up on 28 March 1976 at the former Tilling garage at Catford were RT799, RT501 and RT4771 — the latter a former Country Area bus repainted red at overhaul in 1969.

20

Catford-based RT449 leaves Bromley garage for Shoreditch on 8 July 1973. Route 47 still survives, but the southern terminus is now Catford. Route 47 was one of the last conversions to RM in August 1978 but it had been partially RM-operated since January 1975. Bromley (TB), Catford (TL) and Croydon (TC) were all former Tilling garages.

Left: On 20 July 1974 RT219 stands in the former trolleybus depot at Bexleyheath, which had suffered severe bomb damage as a result of enemy action on 19 June 1944. The depot's trolleybus routes were the 696 and the 698, running in the Dartford/Woolwich area, and these were replaced by RTs in March 1959. Together with the withdrawal of the 654 Crystal Palace–Sutton the same day and the 630 Hammersmith–Croydon route the following year, this left services in the Hammersmith/Kingston/Wimbledon area as the last trolleybus routes in South/West London, and these were the last of all to be withdrawn, in May 1962.

Below: Elmers End garage suffered a direct hit from a flying bomb on 18 July 1944. Apart from some loss of life, 31 service buses were destroyed and another 50 required rebodying. RT1874 was recorded in front of the rebuilt garage on route 54 on 24 September 1972. With the need for public transport apparently diminishing, the garage was closed in 1986.

Left: Standing in the yard of Sidcup garage on 18 March 1973 are three RTs on route 51A — RT3114 (a GB-plated bus), RT939 and RT4076 — while RT1190 was in use as a driver-training bus. In 1988 a self-contained unit known as Bexleybus was introduced from Bexleyheath garage. This operation lasted only three years, but one consequence was the closure of Sidcup garage in 1988.

Above: A line-up on 17 April 1973 outside Walworth garage. This had once been Camberwell tram depot, which was an early casualty of bombing, on 8 September 1940. It was rebuilt and survived as a tram depot until October 1951, when it was rebuilt as a bus garage and renamed Walworth to avoid confusion with the existing Camberwell bus garage. Seen in the photograph are RT2926 on route 176A, RT2177 on route 176 and RM1077 on route 17. The 176 was a tram-replacement route and the 17 an extended trolleybus-replacement route.

A group of RTs stand in Brixton (Telford Avenue) garage — also a former tram depot, the replacing buses arriving at a partly-rebuilt garage in January 1951. From 1936 this depot had been the home of the 'Feltham' tramcars, which operated the 16 and 18 routes between Purley and the Embankment; these routes were replaced in April 1951, the 'Felthams' having been sold to Leeds City Transport. The replacement bus route was the 109, which required no fewer than 88 RTs Mondays to Fridays. Prominent in this view are RT1181 (route 109), RT746 (route 133) and RTs 1162 and 776 both on route 118. RMs took over in 1976.

Another group of RTs — plus an RM — in the yard of Streatham garage on 22 April 1972. This garage was completely rebuilt in 1987 yet closed just five years later.

Left: RT2998 on route 172 passes Tulse Hill Tavern on 29 August 1972. This was a tram-replacement route which was of particular significance, as it brought about closure of the Kingsway Subway. Initially it ran from Highgate to Forest Hill, but in October 1957 the southern terminus was changed to West Norwood. In my extreme youth I have a recollection of short-run buses on route 68 standing in the front of Tulse Hill Tavern. Route 172 forsook its RTs for DMs in 1975.

Above: RT2296, working out of Abbey Wood garage, approaches the terminus of route 180 at Lower Sydenham station on 10 March 1973.

Two years later the route, shared between Catford and Abbey Wood, went over to RM operation. The Abbey Wood share would be operated by MD-class Metropolitans between 1981 and 1983, when the last of these short-lived buses was withdrawn. By that time Plumstead garage had replaced Abbey Wood, the latter garage having closed in 1982. In the same year, the GLC's recently-introduced 'Fares Fair' policy was judged illegal, leading to severe cuts to services, and from 4 September the MDs ceased to work beyond Catford on this route. These cuts also brought about the first normal withdrawals of Routemasters, about 150 being taken out of service as a direct result.

Above: RT1928 on route 94 passes RF129 on LCBS route 402 at Bromley North on 2 July 1976. Of special note is the fact that the 94 held the record for the longest period of continuous RT operation, from 1948 to 1978, when from 27 August RMs took over. This date also saw the end of RTs on route 47, which meant that Bromley and Catford garages lost their last RT routes. The 94 of old is today covered by route 208.

Right: Standing outside Bexleyheath garage on 23 October 1971 are RT1846 and RT4116. Between 1959 and 1962 LT was engaged in the conversion of all trolleybus routes to motor-bus operation. First to change, in March 1959, were the routes in Bexley and Croydon, bus route 96 replacing trolleybus route 696. Bexleyheath garage had been the victim of a flying-bomb attack on 19 June 1944, in which 12 trolleybuses were damaged beyond repair.

Left: Route 57 was a weekdays-only service between Telford Avenue garage and Kingston; the 57A derivative ran only on Sundays, between Stockwell garage and Thornton Heath garage. RT3065 was recorded on the latter route near Streatham Hill on 19 September 1971.

'You wait ages for a bus and then two come along!' RT2981 overtakes
RT1170 on route 54 from Woolwich to West Croydon, at Beckenham
Hospital on 13 July 1976.

Above: RT1107 at Crystal Palace on 19 April 1973. Bus route 154 had replaced trolleybus route 654 in 1959, leading to the closure of the trolleybus garage at Carshalton. RMs would replace the RTs on this route a month after this photograph was taken.

Right: At Crystal Palace Parade opposite the site of the former high-level station (closed in 1954) on 15 May 1977 stand RT1328 on route 122 (converted to RM operation from 1978) and Leyland B15 prototype 004, acting as a demonstrator for what became known as the Titan, on route 3. The 1,125 Titans ordered by LT were delivered from 1978 to 1985; the few survivors work from East London garages and are likely to be withdrawn in 2001.

Working out of Poplar depot and seen near Aldgate bus station on 20 June 1974, RT1708 heads for Herne Hill on route 40A. The feature of this bus was that it then carried the body originally on RT2776, one of the three buses (RT2775 and RTL1307 were the others) that went on a promotional visit to the USA in 1952. RT2776 was used to give rides to the American public, and was fitted with additional ventilators because of the likely warm climates it would encounter. The other two buses were not modified, so this body was unique.

The 76 buses of the RLH class, built between 1950 and 1952, were intended for double-deck routes where low bridges were encountered. To all intents and purposes these were RT-type chassis with Weymann lowbridge bodywork. Most of them worked in the Country Area but 24 were allocated to Central Area duties. RLH57 was recorded in 1970 at Maryland on route 178. This, the last RLH route, was withdrawn in April 1971 to be replaced by single-deck route S2, featuring six Leyland Nationals — the first to enter LT service — and six Metro-Scanias which were not kept for long. *Denis Elliott*

Following successful trials with the four prototypes, Routemasters went into production and from 1958 to 1968 a further 2,756 buses of the RM family were built. One of the earlier buses, RM137, is seen at Westminster on 14 May 1976. The earlier bodies differed in not having opening front windows on the upper deck. At this time route 12 was worked partially out of Elmers End garage.

One would have expected RM8 to be among the earliest to enter service, but in fact it was used as a Chiswick Works test bus and did not enter traffic until 1976. Allocated to Sidcup garage, it was recorded on route 21, approaching London Bridge from the City on 16 May 1976. Note that it carried the LT 'roundel', which by then had replaced the 'LONDON TRANSPORT' fleetnames on all but RTs.

Left: For a short time in the early 1970s about 100 RMs were repainted with an 'open roundel' which had appeared on many of the new DMS buses, but this was to be short-lived. RM1525 stands so adorned in Vauxhall Bridge Road, Victoria, on route 36 on 5 July 1973.

Right: RM1141 passes the Mansion House on route 18 on 15 May 1976. The absence of other traffic and even pedestrians is remarkable. This route crossed Southwark Bridge to reach its London Bridge station terminus. Note that this later RM has opening upper-deck windows as fitted from RM254 onwards.

42

Left: In the 1970s LT went through a phase of applying overall advertising to buses. Few of these were visually attractive, but an exception was RML2701, which received a tartan livery advertising Younger's Scotch Bitter. The bus is seen heading west on route 15 at St Paul's Cathedral on 13 July 1972. It seems that Parliament expressed its dissatisfaction with such liveries, on the grounds that tourists came to London to see red buses.

Right: Approaching its home base, Streatham garage, RM952 was recorded on route 159 on 27 April 1974. This bus advertised Dinky Toys and Meccano. The advertising contracts varied in length, but most were for about two years. Today, many operators overcome the disapproval of overall advertising buses by so painting only the back of the bus, which nevertheless is still a potential distraction to other road users.

In 1961 the Metropolitan Police Authority agreed to the use in the capital of buses of 30ft in length. A preliminary batch of 24 was built (RML880-903), after which construction continued of 27ft 6in RMs. The increased length of the RML enabled 72 passengers to be carried instead of 64. The last RM built was RM2217, after which there was a batch of long 'coaches' for Green Line work, and then RML2261-2760 completed the production run. RML2301 was noted on route 24 in Whitehall on 5 October 1972.

Pausing at an eastbound stop at Ludgate Hill on 5 May 1981, RML2463 and RML2372, both on route 6, are seen with RM2098 on route 11. The Routemasters still to be seen in service in London today are predominantly of the longer RML variety. The blue rail overbridge seen in the background carried the line to Holborn Viaduct station, which closed in 1990. The bridge was demolished the same year as part of preparations for the new Thameslink deviation line.

Left: Another means of advertising was to find sponsors to fund the repainting of buses for special occasions. First and most important of these was the repainting in silver livery of 25 RMs to commemorate HM Queen Elizabeth's Silver Jubilee. These buses were temporarily renumbered in the SRM series; SRM7 on route 25 was recorded in Cheapside in May 1977. It regained its old identity of RM1871 later in the year; all had reverted to red livery by December.

Right: The year 1979 saw the 150th anniversary of London's buses, George Shillibeer having operated a horse-drawn omnibus to carry passengers between Paddington and the Bank in 1829, and, to celebrate this, 14 buses were repainted into an approximation of Shillibeer livery. The year was marked with special events, notably a bus rally which took place in July in Hyde Park, the use of one of the Royal Parks being a special privilege. At Oxford Circus on route 137 on 27 April 1979 were RM2153 in Shillibeer livery and RM2009 in standard red.

Left: Also in 1979 an experimental shoppers' service to the West End was inaugurated with 16 RMs in a distinctive Shoplinker livery. It was launched on 7 April — more widely remembered as the last day in service for the RTs. The Shoplinker service was not a success, and the buses reverted to normal livery in September. RM2139 was noted at Victoria on 24 June.

Above: To commemorate the wedding of HRH Prince Charles and Lady Diana Spencer, eight RMs were painted into a special livery and, as with all these specially-adorned buses, were used on routes that penetrated Central London. RM559 was recorded on route 9 outside the Royal Albert Hall on 21 June 1981.

Left: In 1983 the 50th Anniversary of the formation of the London Passenger Transport Board was celebrated with a special open day at Chiswick Works on 3 July. For this event Leyland Titan T747 and Routemaster RM1983 were specially painted in a gold livery. The latter is seen at Chiswick Works along with RM2217 (the last 27ft 6in Routemaster built), RM2116 (in a special 'General' livery) and RM83.

Above: Following the 1970 takeover of London Transport's Country Area by the National Bus Company, the newly-formed London Country Bus Services placed increased reliance on single-deck buses. As a result, most of its inherited members of the RM family and some RTs were re-purchased by London Transport to offset a shortage of buses due to spares problems and unreliability of the new OMO types. Among the buses which came back into LT stock were the 27ft 6in coach-type Routemasters (RMC1453-1520) built in 1962. The absence of grab rails made them unsuitable for normal service, but they were used on training duties (releasing RMs back into traffic) and as staff buses. RMC1476, a training bus, stands at Bromley garage on 15 May 1981. Some of the RMCs were never put back into use, however, being cannibalised for spare parts.

PRIVATE
To hire a bus or coach
apply. 55 Broadway S.W.1.

DRIVER UNDER
INSTRUCTION

CUV232C

Left: In 1965 LT had put into service 43 30ft coaches (RCL2218-2260), and these too reverted to LT ownership in the late 1970s. As with the RMCs, several of these initially became training buses, including RCL2232, working out of Bow and recorded at Victoria on 3 June 1980. At this time it retained its original twin-headlight arrangement.

Right: Remarkably most of the RCLs were refurbished and put back into passenger service, being shared between Edmonton and Stamford Hill garages, where from 1981 they replaced DM-class Fleetlines and standard RMs on routes 149 and 279 respectively; they continued to perform these duties until 1984. RCL2251 was recorded at Victoria on 15 June 1981. Note that the refurbishment involved the fitment of standard (single) headlamps.

Above left: British European Airways ordered 65 forward-entrance Routemasters to take over the service between the Gloucester Road Air Terminal and Heathrow Airport. These replaced 74 specially-designed coaches of the RF family, which were no longer capable of handling the daily loads experienced. The new Routemasters towed trailers, which enabled passengers' luggage to go straight to or from the aircraft. However, although the RML had been introduced by this time the Ministry of Transport insisted on shorter buses to tow the trailers. Sadly the BEA Routemasters did not run long in their original smart blue and white livery but in 1969 were repainted predominantly orange. BEA11 and BEA15 stand awaiting their turn of duty at Heathrow Airport on 22 May 1974.

Left: In addition to the Routemaster fleet, BEA had eight 'Executive Coach' AEC Reliances, of which EC1 is seen in this line-up at the West London Air Terminal on 16 September 1971. They were sold when the airport service ceased upon opening of the Piccadilly Line extension to Heathrow in 1977.

Above: Routemaster BEA24 stands at Heathrow Airport on 22 May 1974, by now carrying its third livery — British Airways blue and white. These buses operated out of the former Chiswick tram depot, which would later become Stamford Brook garage.

Above: With the Piccadilly Line extension to Heathrow opening in stages, 13 of the BEA Routemasters were released to London Transport in 1975. They were put into traffic at Dalston garage on route 175 — still in BEA colours but sporting the LT roundel. RMA11 (ex-BEA48) is seen at Dagenham on 13 March 1976.

Right: After trials with Atlanteans and Fleetlines, LT decided that its future rear-engined double-decker would be the Fleetline. Classified DMS, the production buses first saw service from 2 January 1971 on routes 220 (originally a trolleybus-replacement route) and 95 (a tram-replacement route), working from Shepherd's Bush and Brixton garages respectively. DMS31 was noted at Streatham Hill on 19 September 1971, its early coin-in-the-slot symbols denoting a 'Pay as you enter' bus.

Left: RT2164 stands at London Bridge station on 15 June 1972 on route 44, which had featured in Stage 1 of the tram-replacement programme. DMS378 should also have been at the stop, but the driver obligingly moved the bus to show the contrast of old and new. In fact route 44 was due to go over to DMS operation on the following Monday, and DMS378 was there to display the type to regular passengers. By this time PAYE was recognised without the need for symbols.

Above: In early 1974, with the new DMS-class buses proving troublesome and with delays in delivery, LT ordered 164 Scania buses with MCW bodywork. These were known as Metropolitans and were classified MD. Initially shared between New Cross and Peckham garages, they were very quiet and smooth in traffic.

MD15, standing apparently empty at Victoria on 31 March 1976, had been delivered a month earlier but incredibly was withdrawn just four years later. RM1261 passes on route 36B, this group of routes being shared between the two types while the MDs were in course of delivery. RMs would return to route 36 as early as January 1980; by September 1980 the New Cross MDs had been moved to Plumstead, and eventually the entire class was stabled there.

59

Left: On delivery from Aldenham to join the allocation at Peckham, MD49 was noted at Baker Street on 17 May 1976. The short life of this class was blamed by LT on 'corrosion problems'; while these were encountered by other operators of the type, it seems more likely LT's disposal of the class had more to do with their being non-standard within the fleet. The MDs were eagerly snapped up by other operators, notably Reading Transport and Whippet Coaches of Fenstanton, the last MD operated by the latter company surviving until 2000! The last had been withdrawn from London service in 1983.

Above: With hindsight, it is a shame that the rear-engined Routemaster, 60% of its components being standard RM parts, was not put into production. Completed in 1966, the prototype, FRM1, entered traffic the following year, by which time LT had made the questionable decision to order high-capacity single-deckers. AEC had been 'merged' with Leyland in 1962, by which time the latter's rear-engined Atlantean — as well as Daimler's Fleetline — was already in production, and AEC's engineers were doubtless dissuaded from continuing with what would have been another rival to Leyland's own model. Furthermore, the 1968 Transport Act stipulated that New Bus Grant would only be given for tried and tested designs.

FRM1 proved a popular bus at Tottenham, where it worked for about two years, chiefly on route 76, but in 1969 it was transferred to Croydon, where LT's 50 Atlanteans were also based. It was standing at Selsdon on route 234B when photographed on 28 August 1971 — rather hurriedly, I might add, because I was driving in the opposite direction!

Left: FRM1 found itself working out of Stockwell garage on the Round London Sightseeing Tour by 1978, at which time the buses so used looked respectable and were not covered with the present-day branding; the bus is seen passing the Merchant Navy War Memorial in Tower Hill. In 1983 FRM1 was withdrawn, but happily it survives in preservation at the Acton depot of the London Transport Museum.

Right: There was a severe shortage of drivers in 1972 and LT could not run the Round London Sightseeing Tour when buses were being cancelled on ordinary routes. Instead it hired five Guy Arabs from the East Kent Road Car Co. These buses appropriately had Park Royal bodies and were built in 1951, being converted to open-top in 1969. Samuelson's New Transport provided drivers, and the buses ran only between June and September. FFN 384 was recorded at St Paul's Cathedral on 13 July 1972.

Left: Private enterprise was also getting in on sightseeing tours. The equally Union Jack-adorned regular bus was an Atlantean of 1961 vintage new to the Standerwick fleet of Ribble Motor Services, but just occasionally the spare bus appeared in the form of the former RT3528, as here in King William Street on 16 September 1971.

Above: In 1965 (when RMLs were still being built) LT bought 50 Leyland Atlanteans of the PDR1/1 type, classified XA. These were initially used as crewed buses on North London routes, where trials took place with XF-class Daimler Fleetlines borrowed from the Country Area; it was these trials that convinced LT to favour the Fleetline for future orders. In 1969 three XAs were transferred to the Country Area in exchange for three RMLs, but the rest moved to Croydon, where they operated as OMO vehicles alongside FRM1; three are seen here at West Croydon on 1 January 1973. All 50 (including the three Country Area buses, which had passed to London Country Bus Services) were sold to China Motor Bus, Hong Kong, later that year.

Left: In September 1975 the fallibility of the MB- and SM-type single-deckers, together with concerns over the poor availability of the DMS fleet, led LT to hire 10 Leyland Titan PD3s from Southend Transport, and these were used on route 190 between Thornton Heath and Old Coulsdon. Remarkably this photograph of Southend 347 near South Croydon on 6 October 1975 also depicts two other PD3s from the same source. The following year saw them on loan to LCBS at Harlow!

Below: Much as it had with the RT, in the early 1950s LT wished to standardise on a single-deck bus and this was the AEC Regal IV, 700 examples being built between 1951 and 1954 and shared between the Central and Country Areas. RF371 on route 218 and RF514 on route 216 stand beside Staines West station on 6 October 1975. The fleet of red RFs amounted to only 225 buses, the majority of the class being Country Area (green) buses or Green Line coaches.

Leaving Hounslow bus station, RF442 heads for Shepperton on route 237 on 25 March 1977. The last RFs were withdrawn two years later, having outlived many of the high-capacity single-deckers. Many have been preserved, including two by the London Transport Museum.

In 1966 LT transferred some routes to private operators because of an overtime ban by drivers, whose union also opposed crews' manning buses for special events or (as seen already) sightseeing tours. One of the routes transferred in 1966 was the short route 235 in Richmond, allocated to Continental Pioneer, which company had a large base on the site of the former railway goods yard. The former RF506 was recorded at Richmond station on 13 July 1978.

Left: Standing outside the former Tilling garage at Croydon, RF483 was observed on 26 November 1972 on route 234B, which involved a relatively short run to Selsdon. Croydon RFs appeared on variations of routes 233 and 234 and were one-man-operated, in common with most RFs in the Central Area.

Above: Most single-deck routes in the London area were numbered in the 2xx series. An exception was route 80, on which RF468 stands outside Sutton garage. This route was also subject to one-man operation (abbreviated to OMO and, later, the more politically-correct OPO). This scene was recorded on 30 August 1971 — probably in the course of a visit to the late John Smith's Len's of Sutton bookshop.

Above: Operation of red RFs came to an end on 30 March 1979, when Kingston routes 218 and 219 were converted to LS (Leyland National) operation from Norbiton, because the new buses were too long to be accommodated at Kingston. RF330 and RF513 with route 215 blinds were recorded at Norbiton garage on 20 January 1974.

Right: In 1965 LT introduced its Reshaping Plan, which, *inter alia*, envisaged a greater use of single-deck buses, some with large standee provision on short journeys, notably the introduction in Central London of the Red Arrow services. The MB-family AEC Swifts (always known as Merlins by LT) were 36ft long, and this created problems in tight turns in busy London streets, but their main failure was unreliability. The production batches entered traffic from 1968, but in 1973 LT decided to replace the type, and two years later most had been withdrawn, 350 being stored out of use at Radlett on a former aerodrome site. In all there were no fewer than 665 members of the MB family, so the decision to place bulk orders with the minimum of road testing was an unhappy one. The MBA variants on Red Arrow services lasted longest, being replaced by Leyland Nationals in 1981. MBA542 was recorded outside Broad Street station on 1 October 1973. The former North London Railway Broad Street terminus was closed in 1986 and demolished to make way for the Broadgate development.

73

Very much away from its usual haunts, MBA535 was a rare sight passing through the toll gate administered by the Dulwich College Estates on Sunday 24 October 1976. It was very unusual for a railway-replacement service to take this route, which was dictated by subsidence in Croxted Road. Ordinary bus services had to make a longer diversion.

Another drawback with the Merlins was that their 36ft length occupied too much garage space. Hence an order was placed for 838 similar buses of 33ft length — the SM family. Built from 1969 to 1972, these were more manœuvrable but had a less powerful engine, which brought further problems. They had slightly longer working lives than most of the MB family, but all had been taken out of traffic by 1981. SMS636 was recorded on route A1, which ran non-stop between Heathrow Airport and Hounslow West station, on 22 May 1974. This service was withdrawn in December 1977 on completion of the Piccadilly Line to Heathrow Central; for its final 15 months it had been operated by Leyland Nationals.

Left: Still bearing its PAYE symbols, SMS433 climbs the hill from Chislehurst station to Crystal Palace on route 227. This had been worked by RFs until 1971 and would be taken over by Leyland Nationals in 1977. This scene was recorded on 12 November 1973.

Right: The Leyland National, once ubiquitous in fleets around the country, might be described as London Transport's first successful 'off the peg' bus. Apart from a rear route number and moquette seating no modifications were made to the type for London service. The first six, placed in service by LT in 1973, were used on route S2 (covering much of the former RLH route 178), and six Metro-Scanias were purchased for comparative purposes. With the lamentable failure of its previous single-deck buses, LT soon ordered more, and the Nationals became the standard large-capacity single-decker, the LS class eventually amounting to 506 buses. Route 138, operated from Bromley garage, was converted to National operation in 1979; LS374 is seen in suitably spring-like conditions near Hayes on 16 April 1981.

Left: The first of the Metro-Scanias, MS1, running trials in the Central Area, shadowing a Routemaster on route 11 at Victoria on 18 June 1973. The conversion of route S2 (Clapton Pond–Bromley-by-Bow) to LS and MS operation did not take place until 13 August, on which day MS4 disgraced itself by diverting *into* Clapton Pond, fortunately with little damage. The Metro-Scanias lasted on the route only until June 1976. MS2 was later used as an experimental bus, ultimately being preserved; the others were sold to Newport Transport, where they joined 44 similar buses.

Above: The Leyland National 2 was quite distinctive in having a front-mounted radiator. In 1980 LT took delivery of 69 examples to replace the MBAs on Red Arrow services. This scene was recorded at Victoria on 22 June 1981, by which time the process should have been completed. The buses on route 500 are MBA531 and LS486.

Index of Locations

In 1975 the first six (of 17) BS-class ECW-bodied Bristol LHS types were purchased to replace Ford Transit minibuses on GLC-subsidised route C11, then recently introduced. The following year the first of 95 BL-class standard-length Bristol LH/ECW buses arrived; seating 39, these were comparable in size to the RFs, which they replaced on many routes, including the 80 and 80A from Sutton garage. BL28 was recorded near Burgh Heath on 22 August 1976, apparently admired by the Riley family.